# LET YOUR LIGHT SHINE!

An Evangelism Training Program for Those
Who Want to Share the Savior with Others

STEPHEN KURTZAHN

Text Copyright © 2012 Stephen C. F. Kurtzahn
All Rights Reserved

Scripture taken from the New King James
Version ®
Copyright © 1982 by Thomas Nelson, Inc.
Used by permission
All rights reserved

*Philip found Nathanael and said to him, "We have found Him of whom Moses in the law, and also the prophets, wrote; Jesus of Nazareth, the son of Joseph." And Nathanael said to him, "Can anything good come out of Nazareth?" Philip said to him, "Come and see!"* John 1:45, 46

# TABLE OF CONTENTS

LESSON ONE: A DEFINITION — Page 1

LESSON TWO: THE BIBLICAL BASIS — Page 7

LESSON THREE: OUR AREA OF RESPONSIBILITY — Page 14

LESSON FOUR: MISCONCEPTIONS, OBSTACLES AND EXCUSES — Page 20

LESSON FIVE: PASSIVE EVANGELISM — Page 27

LESSON SIX: ACTIVE EVANGELISM — Page 34

LESSON SEVEN: FITTING EVANGELISM INTO YOUR EVERYDAY LIFE — Page 41

LESSON EIGHT: RESPONDING TO EXCUSES — Page 50

LESSON NINE: ASSIMILATING THE NEW MEMBER — Page 56

# INTRODUCTION

A young girl woke up in a cold, clammy sweat in the middle of the night. She had suffered a terrible nightmare. What did she dream that made her so afraid? All the people of the world were running wildly headlong down a wide road like a herd of stampeding cattle. The road stopped, much to her horror, at the edge of a steep cliff. She was the only one who could stop the multitude from plunging downward to certain death. What was she to do? The little girl didn't know, but when she thought of all the people who didn't know Jesus, chills went up and down her spine.

A middle-aged businessman came to his pastor's study one day. The minister could sense that something was wrong. The gentleman in the gray, pinstriped suit had been very successful in his work. He also had an excellent home life with his family. So what was wrong that he so desperately needed to see the pastor? In his dealings with business associates he discovered many who had no religious beliefs, and who lived life without direction, hope or meaning. How greatly his heart yearned to share the message of the Savior, who forgives sin and imparts eternal life! But every time he opened his mouth to say something about Jesus, he suddenly found himself tongue-tied.

The church council of a Christian congregation in a middle-class community came to the stark realization that every church in town had grown — but theirs! It would have been very easy to be complacent about the whole thing, but these God-fearing individuals were concerned — concerned because they knew they had the Gospel of Christ! They had in their possession that wonderful Word which brought peace to the soul. But they just didn't know how to get God's Word out into their community.

If you are concerned that people you know will not be in heaven when they die....If you realize your own weaknesses and failings when it comes to sharing the Gospel with others....If you want people to come to your church because of its message and not its social programs....then this study course hopes to aid you in your endeavors. It does not pretend to be the last word in evangelism.

It does hope to offer the reader the scriptural basis for witnessing and some tools to use in order to carry out that witness in our normal, everyday lives.

May the Lord Jesus, the Chief Shepherd of the Church, richly bless your study and your efforts!

# LESSON ONE: A DEFINITION

If you would ask ten people who consider themselves "Christian" to give their own definition of the word "evangelism," you would probably receive ten different answers. When one hears the word "evangelism," Billy Sunday of years gone by might come to mind, or Billy Graham and his huge evangelistic crusades.

Some believe that "evangelism" is done best when you stand out on a street corner and hand out religious tracts. In some parts of the United States self-made preachers evangelize in parking lots with very loud Public-Address systems. Still others feel that to be an "evangelist" you must approach every person you meet with the question, "Are you saved?"

On the other side of the coin we have a large number of people who think "evangelism" is best accomplished through social activism. How often haven't we heard it said, "You must fill a person's stomach before he will want to feed on the Bread of Life?" As a result of this kind of philosophy, many denominations spend their mission money mostly on the relief of world hunger, injustice and poverty. Yes, the Lord wants us to love our neighbor, but is that what is properly called "evangelism?"

What is "evangelism?" To answer this question simply and plainly we must go back to the original language in which our New Testament was written. Our English word "evangelize" comes from a Greek word that literally means, "TO PROCLAIM GOOD NEWS." Cf. Luke 9:6; 1 Corinthians 1:17; Acts 8:25; Luke 7:22; Acts 14:7.

We see then that to "evangelize" means simply to proclaim Good News—the Good News that the Savior has come who has removed the curse of sin and has clothed us in robes of righteousness. This Good News brings light, joy and peace to guilt-ridden hearts, for they have come to trust the Lamb of God, Jesus Christ, John 1:29.

Before we go on to study the Biblical reasons why we should "evangelize," we must realize three things—

1) The Bible does not tell us that we must use

a certain method to bring the Good News to others.  At Jacob's well the Master casually brought in the fact that He is the Water of Life in a normal, everyday conversation, John 4:1-26.  When He gave His magnificent Sermon on the Mount, Jesus sat on a hill so all could hear, even though He was addressing His disciples, Matthew 5:1-2.  He taught in homes and along the seashore.  If Jesus would have come to save humanity in our day, He very likely would have used radio, television, dvd's, the Internet, texting and many other technological advances, Mark 2:1-2; Mark 4:1.

2) We must always remember that "evangelism" consists ONLY of proclaiming the Good News of the Redeemer.  Feeding the poor, caring for the needy, bringing people into the church by means of its social and recreational programs, is not "evangelism" in the Scriptural sense of the word.  What this world needs most of all, especially in our day and age, is a knowledge of our Savior's love, a love so great that it cost Him His life.  If the church is concerned only with taking care of people's physical needs, who is left to give them the life-giving Word?  Cf. Matthew 28:19-20.

3) We do not evangelize in order to build up the visible church on earth with a great number of people.  We do not preach the Gospel to increase our membership lists.  We share the Good News of divine love so that those around us may know the only true God, and Jesus Christ, whom He has sent, John 17:3.  Our primary purpose for doing mission work, whether at home in the United States or abroad in a foreign country, is to bring the Savior's forgiveness to those sitting in darkness, Mark 16:15.  Involvement in a church, among a group of believers, follows in order that these new Christians may continue growing in the Word of God, John 8:31-32; John 15:9.

THINGS TO DO BEFORE THE NEXT LESSON

1) Pray for your pastor, your congregation, your church body, and your own evangelism efforts.  Ask the heavenly Father to bless us as we endeavor to reach out to others with the Gospel.

2) Keep your eyes open during the coming week, and try to count how many times God

opens up opportunities for you to share the Gospel.

3) Make a list of people who, as far as you know, are not regular attendees of a Christian church. Consider this your personal Responsibility List. Add to it each week. Pray for these people by name.

DISCUSSION QUESTIONS

1) What is the basic meaning of the word "evangelism?"

2) What is the main purpose behind our evangelism efforts?

3) What message, and what message only, is to be proclaimed to those outside of the Church?

4) How have many churches failed in their evangelism efforts?

5) Why should people be invited to church and encouraged to become members?

6) Give some examples of how we can use

modern technology in our mission work.

7) How should we look on those people who do not yet know in faith the forgiveness of Jesus?

# LESSON TWO: THE BIBLICAL BASIS

Why should we spend our precious time in prayer for our unchurched friends and relatives? What is so important about living the God-pleasing life so those around us will take notice? Why does Jesus want us to tell others of His love and forgiveness? Why must we always keep our eyes open for opportunities to witness?

Let's imagine for a moment that you live in a large metropolitan area, such as Los Angeles, Chicago or New York. You discover that a terrorist organization was going to poison the water supply of your city. You are the only person who knows about it. Wouldn't you inform the proper authorities, so that the lives of millions of people could be saved?

## GOD'S ANGER OVER SIN

Our work of evangelism, or "preaching the Good News," is just as important as the example given above. In fact, it is MORE important than anything else in this whole world. For if people don't have the chance to hear what Jesus did for them, if they don't have the opportunity for the Spirit to work faith in Jesus in their hearts, they will suffer in the eternal torments of hell. There is nothing in hell but weeping and gnashing of teeth, Matthew 25:30; Romans 10:13-17.

People don't like to talk about hell anymore. In fact, a lot of pastors don't mention it in their sermons and a lot of churches fail to write about it in their periodicals and devotionals these days. So how can we dare paint such a gloomy picture for unconverted mankind? The Bible itself speaks of such eternal anguish.

When the almighty Creator placed Adam and Eve in the Garden of Eden, He gave them specific orders not to eat of the tree of knowledge of good and evil. But being prodded by the devil in the form of a snake, the man and woman both ate of the tree, Genesis 3:1-7. From that moment on man had lost God's image. He became spiritually dead, was doomed to die physically, and, unless redeemed by the blood of Jesus Christ, would suffer in hell forever both in body and soul, Genesis 2:17; Genesis 5:3.
Many hundreds of years later, after the Garden of Eden incident, the Lord Jehovah

gave to His people Israel the Torah, or Law, on Mount Sinai. These are instructions for proper living which the Creator gave to men so we would realize how utterly condemnable we are in His sight. In fact, God demands that we be holy, Leviticus 11:44, 45, but that is totally impossible for us.

The disobedience to God's will as it is revealed in the Law is what we commonly call "sin." In the Scriptures, the word "sin" has several different connotations. It may refer to the sinner's "act of rebellion" — just as a child may detest the commands of it parents, so people deliberately do the opposite of what God wants. At other times sin is pictured as a "debt," or a "load of guilt" which must be repaid or removed if the sinner is ever to live in the Lord's presence. And still, at other times, sin is illustrated as a "missing of the mark."

What are the results of such sin, or any sin, for that matter? To put it simply: DEATH. In our natural state of iniquity, we are as walking corpses before God, Ephesians 2:1. As murderers are subject to life in prison or even to the death penalty, even so has the divine

Judge demanded payment and retribution for breaking His laws, Galatians 3:10.

GOD'S LOVE FOR THE SINNER

Why God planned our salvation, we'll never be able to figure out with our human minds. Why He gave us a way of escape from His eternal wrath is simply too wonderful — too overwhelming — for us to comprehend. But out of a love which knows no limits, the Lord saved us unworthy sinners from eternal punishment. He supplies us with His salvation through His Son. The message of how Jesus saved lost humanity is called the Gospel. This is the Good News which must be preached throughout the far reaches of the globe, Mark 16:15.

On Mount Sinai God not only threatened punishment for disobedience but He also demanded obedience. Jesus took care of both things for us. As our Representative represents us, the voters of his district, in Congress, so Jesus represents the whole human race before His heavenly Father. By His perfect life, His holiness, His sinlessness, His purity, Jesus covered over all our disobedience. Remember—Christ is our Substitute and Representative. So when God looks upon us, He sees Christ. When He sees us, He sees His beloved Son, in whom He is well pleased. Cf. Romans 5:19.

But God is just. Payment had to be made for our sins. As Judge, He simply could not overlook our iniquity, any more than an earthly judge can release a convicted murderer because he promises to be good. But again, Jesus Christ steps into the picture. As our Substitute, Christ endured the divine punishment in our place upon the cross. While He hung there on Calvary, Jesus suffered the very pains of hell which we deserved to suffer in all eternity. Cf. Romans 3:25; 2 Corinthians 5:21; 1 John 2:2.

It is exactly this message of the Savior which men, women and children need to hear today. There is only one way to heaven, and that is through Jesus Christ our Lord. And there is only one way that faith in the Redeemer can be created in the human heart—through the Means of Grace, the Gospel in Word and Sacraments. Men and women cannot "decide" on their own to believe, for they are dead in their trespasses and sins. The faith which we have in our hearts is the gift of the Holy Spirit, and this Spirit works only through the Means of Grace. Cf. Ephesians 2:8, 9; Romans 10:17.

So you can see then why "evangelism" is so important. It offers life and salvation to people lost in darkness and death. Just sit back and think about it for a moment — SALVATION! Not only through Christ's life and suffering and death and resurrection are people put in a right relationship with their Maker, but they have life — eternal life. We are not just speaking here of the immortality of the soul — even pagans believe that. But what we are talking about is a resurrected life, when our bodies will be raised from their graves and we will walk and talk and live with Jesus forever. This is the fruit of Christ's redemptive work. This is the result of our Savior's resurrection on Easter. "Because I live, so shall you also live!" If only all people would hear and believe the Good News!

THINGS TO DO BEFORE THE NEXT LESSON

1) Continue to pray for your pastor, your

congregation, your church body, and your own evangelism efforts.

2) Continue updating your personal Responsibility List. Pray for these unchurched people regularly.

3) In your conversations with others this week, try to keep your ears open for a cry for help. Despair, a fear of death, a confused outlook on life, and uncertainty about the future are all signs of anguish under a heavy load of guilt.

4) On a sheet of paper, write out for yourself a Law and Gospel presentation. Write out what you yourself would say to a person who did not know Christ by faith. Use your own words, but make sure you show WHY we deserve God's wrath, and HOW Jesus delivered and saved us from that wrath.

## LESSON THREE: OUR AREA OF RESPONSIBILITY

If you are familiar with the Book of Acts you know that it records for us the spread of the Gospel throughout the world. It tells how thousands were converted to Christianity on the Day of Pentecost, Acts 2:41. We read how evangelists, such as Philip, proclaimed the Good News in Samaria and to an Ethiopian Eunuch, Acts 8. We are overwhelmed by the account of Saul's conversion, who was changed by Christ from a persecutor of the church into the great apostle to the Gentiles, after that known as Paul.

At the end of Matthew's Gospel, sometime during the forty days after Easter, Jesus commanded His disciples to "go" and "make disciples of all nations," Matthew 28:19. St. Luke, the author of Acts, fills us in on some of the conversation between Christ and His followers on the last day He was visibly among them. We read in Acts 1:8 that our glorious and resurrected Lord told His disciples, "...Ye shall be witnesses of Me in Jerusalem, and in all Judea, and in Samaria, and unto the uttermost parts of the earth."

The remainder of the Book tells how the ascended Lord accomplished this through His disciples.

## CHRISTIANS WITH A GLOBAL OUTLOOK

Our Lord's command to "make disciples of all nations" still stands. We, the Christians of the 21st Century, are to reach out to all people with the love of the Savior: those who are both near and far. In order to aid us in understanding our role as evangelists, we need to realize that we are Christians with a "global outlook." Just as the first believers witnessed in Jerusalem and Judea, so we can share Jesus with those in our community and state. As they went into Samaria with the Gospel, so can we in neighboring states and countries. And as the Word of the Lord grew into the uttermost parts of the Roman Empire, so we can reach the heathen through a workable mission program.

## HOW WE IMPLEMENT OUR GLOBAL OUTLOOK AND CONCERN

We have endeavored in various ways to share the Great Message of Scripture with those in our communities. New missions are sprouting up all the time here in the United States. We are also reaching out into the world through our foreign mission program.

Notice one thing, however. All the work we have mentioned is done through the ORGANIZATION. Some have been known to say that organizations are a "necessary" evil. Why are they necessary? Local churches must be incorporated to conduct business. We need a church council to oversee the affairs of the congregation. We gather together with like-minded believers into synods, so our youth can be educated, so we can have a constant supply of pastors and teachers, and so funds can be gathered for mission endeavors.

But, as we said before, organizations are a necessary "evil."

Let's explain. Many individual Christians feel that their responsibility for mission work ceases when they place their "mission" offering in the collection plate. "Why should I go out and speak to others about my religion when I can conveniently put a check in the plate and have others do the work for me?" "Why should I take the time to tell my neighbor about divine forgiveness when the pastor is getting paid to do it?"

If we want to carry out the Great Commission which the Savior has given to us, we must realize the responsibility our Lord has placed upon us as individuals. When Christ says "Go," He's not just speaking to synods and church bodies, but to individual people. When He commands us to preach the Gospel "to every creature," He has in mind that aunt or uncle or cousin; that brother or sister or father or mother; your neighbor or boss or the person who works next to you. With whomever we come into contact, Jesus wants us to share His divine peace and hope.

## AN ENCOURAGEMENT

In order to make ourselves realize how important evangelism really is, let's get into the habit of viewing people as Jesus does: they are the ones for whom He died and shed His blood. If we don't tell them the Good News, who will? And if not now, when?

Such thoughts might scare us, and the responsibility towards those we know might be too great to humanly handle. But remember this story of a man who was once a missionary to India. Whenever he thought of the millions of people in that country still blinded by paganism, he would throw up his hands in near despair. He would pray, "I can't do it all, Lord!" But then he came to a marvelous realization as he studied God's Word—it wasn't all up to him. He just had to share the Means of Grace, the Gospel in Word and Sacrament, and the Holy Spirit would do the rest. What a comforting thought for us to remember, as each of us personally works with our fellow human beings with the Word!

THINGS TO DO BEFORE THE NEXT LESSON

1) Continue to pray for your pastor, your church body, your congregation and your own evangelism efforts.

2) Continue to update your Personal Responsibility List.

3) Continue to review and practice your Law

and Gospel presentation.

# LESSON FOUR: MISCONCEPTIONS, OBSTACLES AND EXCUSES

In the past few lessons we have seen what the word "evangelism" means from a Scriptural viewpoint. We examined how evangelism fits into the total framework of the church. The Message we are to proclaim was considered. And we spoke how we should share that Word with people we are in contact with every day.

What we have covered so far could be called our "Biblical foundation." We have seen for ourselves what God, in His Word, has to say about the "who, what, why and when" of evangelism. All we have left to consider is the "how." Holy Scripture has a great deal to say about this, too. How do we witness? What tools can be used? What advice can be offered?

Before we dig into the answers to such questions, we should look at several things which might hinder us in our work as evangelists. After we realize what kind of misconceptions, obstacles and excuses might cross our way, it is very possible that we can avoid them.

## MISCONCEPTIONS

"THE PASTOR IS TO DO ALL THE MISSION WORK." You would not believe how many people actually think this. If you yourself have thought this way, you couldn't be more mistaken! It is true, a pastor is to be about doing mission work, but his first concern is in serving the congregation to which he has been called by God. In large churches there are meetings several nights a week. And whether it is a large church or a small one, the pastor has sermons to prepare, Bible classes to get ready, sick calls to make, counseling sessions to arrange, visits to members and shut-ins, mailings to prepare, Bible instruction classes to conduct; and if there is no secretary, bulletins and mailings to produce. Plus he needs to spend time with his family. And then he alone is expected to go out and do all the mission work?

"THE UNCHURCHED CAN COME HERE." Lazy pastors put it this way: "If someone wants to see me, or come to church, he knows where the door is!" The only way we can respond to such an attitude is to ask, "Who's going to come and see the pastor? Who's going to step through the doors of the church?" Unbelievers are "dead in their trespasses and sins," Ephesians 2:1. They do not realize their lost condition until their consciences are prodded by the Law, and they don't know their Savior from sin until they taste the sweetness of the Gospel. Why would a person, who does not recognize such things, want to spend an hour or two on Sunday morning in church when there are so many other things to do?

"WE EVANGELIZE IN ORDER TO INCREASE OUR MEMBERSHIP." You could put this statement another way: "We evangelism to increase our Sunday school enrollment." Or, "We evangelize to boost our offerings." Such an opinion is selfish as well as dangerous. It is selfish, because then we would be looking for people to serve the congregation, instead of the congregation looking for people it can serve. It is also dangerous in two very serious respects: 1) It makes us think that membership in the visible church is more important than membership in the Holy Christian Church. We tend to feel that having our names recorded on a church membership roster is better than having them written in heaven in the Book of Life. 2) Such a thought is also dangerous because it can so easily lead to gimmickry. Our overriding concern then becomes more members — and we end up catering to all sorts of social needs just to fill the pews of the church. Now there is nothing wrong with having fellowship activities among believers, but if we use such things to gain more members, we must ask ourselves if we have lost the Gospel and are trying to offer cheap substitutes.

OBSTACLES

What are some of the barricades which prevent us from doing mission work as the Lord wants us to? The first obstacle may be not praying enough. A great deal can be accomplished through prayer, and how might things go better for us all, if we would take our concerns to Jesus first, rather than saving prayer as a last resort?

When it comes to prayer, let's recall our Savior's words, "I will do whatever you ask in My name," John 14:13. Let's also remember

Dr. Martin Luther. When asked how he could accomplish so much in one day, he responded by saying that he spent several hours each morning in prayer. Several hours! How long do we spend?

Another obstacle which prevents us from doing mission work as we should is this opinion: "We don't expect or plan to grow." Also tied in with this thought is pessimism. We may not feel good about ourselves. We may not honestly believe that our church and church body will grow. We become pessimistic when we remember the controversies and religious battles of the past. The pessimistic person looks only for more unhappy things to come, and has no vision or plan for the future. In truth, the pessimistic person shows a weakness of faith in our Lord who says in His Word, "With God all things are possible," Matthew 19:26.

EXCUSES

The Christian who is full of misconceptions about evangelism and who runs into many obstacles in his mission work will usually excuse himself from speaking to anyone about the Savior and His forgiveness. Let's see what some of the more common excuses are—

"IT JUST ISN'T DONE IN OUR CHURCH." The person who says this quite possibly was turned off by the outreach efforts of the sects or the fanatics. But such an attitude makes us then ask, "What is church for?" Is it a local club, whose membership is limited to only a certain select few? Or is it a social group, to which people come to be entertained? Or is church an opportunity where even the worse sinners can come and hear God's Word and find rest for their burdened souls? The way we look at OUR church will influence greatly our opinions about evangelism and how we assimilate new members (more on this in the final chapter).

"WE DON'T SPEAK TO OTHERS ABOUT RELIGION." Some put it this way, "When I talk to people, there are two subjects I avoid — politics and religion!" If we have no hesitation to speak to our neighbor about where to get the best buys on lettuce or motor oil, why can't we tell them about the greatest "bargain" of all—free salvation in Jesus Christ?

"I DON'T HAVE THE GIFT." This is the real "cop-out." Has this individual really tried? We don't discover God-given talents in our children until they have been in school for many years. Are we going to give up after witnessing only once or twice?

THINGS TO DO BEFORE THE NEXT LESSON

1) Continue to pray for your pastor, your congregation, your church body, and your own evangelism efforts.

2) Continue to pray for those unchurched people on your personal responsibility list.

3) Analyze your own inhibitions and hang-ups when it comes to evangelism. Do they fall into any of the categories listed above?

4) Speak to someone you know about the Savior. Try at least once every week for the next month. See if you can begin to feel more comfortable with witnessing.

# LESSON FIVE: PASSIVE EVANGELISM

During the past few weeks as we have been digesting the material in this evangelism training program entitled, LET YOUR LIGHT SHINE!, I'm sure you have asked yourself, "When will we start with the practical aspects of mission work?" Now that we have covered the materials which deal with the Biblical basis for witnessing, we can begin our study of "how" to do mission work. We divide this into two sections—passive evangelism and active evangelism. Passive evangelism consists in what the congregation can do to make itself more visible in the community. Active evangelism consists of what individuals can do personally to share their faith in Christ with others on a one-to-one basis.

## LET PEOPLE KNOW WHERE YOU ARE!

The first thing a church must do is to let people know it exists, and where it is located. In small towns this is not difficult, unless the church is on a small side street which does not have much traffic. In a large city, this task can prove to be much more difficult, no matter where the location of the building might be.

How does a congregation remedy such a situation? The first place to start is with the setting up of signs — one large attractive one in front of the church, and several directional signs on adjacent main streets.

When new businesses start up in a community, and they want to be known and recognized, they advertise — not only on billboards, but also on radio, television, in newspapers and on Internet websites. For many of us, the costs of TV are prohibitive, but radio can be used effectively if it is used properly. Sometimes radio stations offer free public service announcements for churches and other non-profit organizations. Some congregations have made good use of paid radio time by broadcasting 30 second devotions each morning.

By far, the newspaper is the one media source used most by churches. Each week special stories are published on what the churches in the community are doing. On any Friday or Saturday, you can find a listing of churches in a special church directory section in most of our newspapers. But advertising in a newspaper can very often lose its effectiveness. An ad can get lost in a clutter of other ads.

Another method churches have used effectively is the sending out of a church information pamphlet to new residents in a community. Monthly listings of new residents can be purchased from a variety of sources. With this little attractive piece of paper, a church hopes to show people where it is located; but most important, it wants to get its message across. In producing a church information pamphlet, several things must be remembered — 1) The wording must be brief and concise. People will not seriously look at something in their door or mailbox that cannot be glanced at and read in a few seconds. 2) The pamphlet must be illustrated. Religious pictures also communicate a message, plus they attract attention. 3) The pamphlet must be produced in a professional manner. Sloppy typing, typographical errors, etc., do not speak well of a group of believers entrusted with the Means of Grace. Besides, we don't want people turned off by such things before they even come and visit our services!

## WHAT WE HAVE TO OFFER

People need to know what message a church has to proclaim, just as much as they need to know where it is located. This need can also be filled with the church information pamphlet. It can contain a simple Law and Gospel message, which relates the love of the Savior to fallen sinners who might otherwise never hear of Christ's forgiveness.

## FOLLOW UP

With the sending out of such materials, there hopefully will be many names crossing over the pastor's desk. But just one contact with such people is not enough. Follow up must be made and pursued. In order to do this, all names of new residents should be kept on file and up to date. After the first pamphlet is sent out, newsletters should be distributed on a regular basis. We hope such an effort will keep reminding people who we are, what we teach, and where we are located.

OUR GOAL

What do we hope to accomplish with all this work? When people, especially new residents, think of a Lutheran church, we want them to think of ours. When a problem or difficulty arises in their lives, we want them to know they can find comfort and guidance from God's Word here. If people desire a thoroughly Christian and Bible-centered education for their children, we want them to think of our Sunday School or our Lutheran elementary school. If someone is looking for our church on Sunday morning, we want them to know exactly where we are located.

MUCH MORE WORK TO DO

Through many different polls, surveys and questionnaires, it has been determined that only about ten percent of all new members first visit a church because of such efforts that we have mentioned above. This is a small figure indeed, but it is a start. And once Christians get serious about the organized evangelism efforts of their own congregation, they will be more encouraged and motivated to witness on their own.

THINGS TO DO BEFORE THE NEXT LESSON

1) Continue to pray for your pastor, your congregation, your church body, and your own evangelism efforts.

2) At least once each week, beginning this week, give someone you know a copy of your church's information pamphlet. After the person has received it, pray that God the Holy Spirit will work in his or her heart by means of the Word of God which it contains.

3) If you speak to someone about your church, be sure to emphasize that it proclaims the Savior's love and forgiveness. Also be sure they know where your church is located, so they don't confuse your church with another.

4) Volunteers could —

a. Find out which radio stations in the area have free public service announcements for churches, and which stations have the lowest advertising rates.

b. Place posters in various locations for the church in your community.

c. Organize a day when many of your members will be able to go out and place pamphlets in various neighborhoods.

# LESSON SIX: ACTIVE EVANGELISM

In the last chapter we centered our attention on "passive" evangelism—what the congregation can do as a whole in order to make itself visible within the community. We discussed several things, such as advertising and public awareness. Today, we want to consider the other side of the witnessing coin: "active" evangelism. What can we actively do as individuals to share our faith with others?

## HOW DO WE START?

Our Lord Jesus knew people inside and out. He knew exactly what to say to someone and how and when to say it. He knew if someone needed to hear about God's wrath over sin, or God's love for the sinner. John 2:24, 25 says that Jesus "knew all men, and had no need that anyone should testify of man, for He knew what was in man."

With us, however, things are different. We are not omniscient like our Redeemer. We need to learn to understand people and be able to recognize their wants and needs and desires if we are to share the Gospel in a relevant way.

So how should we view others? First of all, people need to be loved, recognized and accepted. It's a medical fact that if newborn babies are not touched, held and loved, they will soon die. It is no different with adults and growing children. Even those rugged individuals who give the appearance that they want to be left alone need other people. God, in His divine wisdom, recognized this during Creation Week when He formed Eve, the first woman, Genesis 2:18.

Secondly, people have spiritual, as well as physical needs. Whether they recognize it or not, people have a spiritual side to their nature. This truth is evident among the heathen, who search for God in their idol worship. The triune God has given evidence of Himself in nature, and to man an inner desire to search after Him. But we don't know who He is, or how He has saved us, except in the Bible. Cf. Acts 17:16-34; Romans 1:18-20; Romans 2:14, 15.

Thirdly, people are sinful. Above all, they are in need of the Savior's forgiveness. Visit any mental health clinic or hospital, and you will soon discover that a great deal of mental illness is brought about by feelings of severe guilt. By nature people are not in a right relationship with their heavenly Father. They fall far short of God's demands as revealed in the Ten Commandments. They are under the wrath of almighty God, and, unless they have Christ's forgiveness through faith, are headed to an eternity of misery in hell.

In a world of uncertainty, violence, immorality and death, people need to know above all else that JESUS LOVES THEM! He takes us as we are, no matter how cold or bad or wicked we may be. The Son of God shed His blood to forgive us and make us His own. What we want to do is simply share this Good News with those who so desperately need it!

PRELIMINARIES IN THE WITNESSING PROCESS

There was a time when many Christians thought witnessing consisted of approaching a person on the street and asking him if he was saved. If the answer was "no," the evangelist would back the fellow into a corner and preach a sermon.

But more and more people are beginning to realize that witnessing is best accomplished in an atmosphere of trust and confidence. What better way is there than to share your faith over a cup of coffee, or a Coke, or lunch, with friends who have come to know you and trust you? There are several things which are necessary to build such relationships.

1. TAKE AN INTEREST IN PEOPLE. When our Lord lived among us here on earth, going about His work of saving lost mankind, He took a very deep and personal interest in people — the newly married couple who ran out of wine at their wedding, the woman at the well who was rejected by the "respectable" citizens of her community, the tax collector who was hated by his countrymen, the weeping widow of Nain, the beggar, the leper, the man on the cross next to Him. Jesus was very well aware of their feelings and needs, and He was always ready to help them.

If we want to follow our Master's example as we carry out our Gospel witness, we will take a sincere interest in the boys and girls playing ball, the sales lady at the grocery store, the mailman, the barber, the hairdresser, the family next door, the person next to you at work.

2. LEARN TO KNOW THEM. If you really want to help a person in his relationship with the Savior, you will want to get to know him. You should get past the barriers which he has erected and the mask he has put on. You will want to learn things about him — his work, his family life, his standards, goals and ideals, as well as his problems and needs. The more you learn about a person, the better prepared you will be to relate the Good News of Jesus to his own personal life.

3. ACCEPT THEM. Always be ready to accept a person, even when his ideas, goals and outlooks are different than your own. We must realize that people have a right to their own opinions, even when they are different from our own. To accept a person does not mean that you agree with him.

4. BE READY TO HELP. When people come to the realization that you care about them and accept them, they will often open up to you and tell you of the things which are

troubling them. They may tell you about a son or daughter who is having a problem at school or with some friends. A family member may be sick. Someone is out of work. Another is having emotional difficulties. Feelings of loneliness, despair, or anguish frequently arise.

When people do open up to us, it is because they trust us and are confident that we might be able to help. What a marvelous open door we then have to say a word about our Savior, with His divine, compassionate and forgiving love!

EXERCISE

In order to help us understand what the caring, accepting and sympathetic individual is like, we will consider several people — "make believe," of course, and somewhat exaggerated to make a point. Tell if their witnessing efforts are in accord with what we learned today. Give a reason for your answer. Also tell how their behavior could be improved.

1) Mary is a gossip. She cannot keep a secret.

She always betrays the confidence of her friends, and she tells people at work about the shortcomings of her fellow church members. After gossiping with a neighbor one day, Mary invites her to church.

2) Sam is a quite man, who only speaks to grumble and complain. His language is always salted with profanity, and he loves to make his acquaintances feel bad by always telling them what they do wrong. After listening to a sermon on witnessing during a mission festival, he gets up the courage to tell a co-worker about the Savior.

3) Joe is an average sort of guy, but well liked by all who know him. He has his faults, but he readily admits them. He speaks well of everyone he knows, and works hard at his job. Talking to a co-worker at lunch, Joe hears the sad story of a man burdened with guilt because he cheated on his wife and is now suffering through a divorce. Joe proceeds to tell him of how Jesus forgives the worst of sinners.

# LESSON SEVEN: FITTING EVANGELISM INTO YOUR EVERYDAY LIFE

## OPEN DOORS

Our lesson from the previous chapter, which dealt with the preliminaries of the witnessing process, could be summarized in three short and simple words—"BE A FRIEND." When an unchurched person, or even one who goes to church regularly, discovers that you accept him, know him and are sincerely interested in him, he will open up to you. In his every day conversations with you he will speak out about certain problems and concerns he has. As he learns to trust you he will sometimes pour out his heart to you because he feels you might have something to offer to help him. Such opportunities are open doors which the Lord Himself opens up for us so we can share the Good News of forgiveness, peace and eternal life in Christ.

## SOME ADVICE

When we tell others about Jesus and His forgiving love, it is very easy to speak of our own experiences and our own ideas. We are all familiar with "testimonials," when people tell us we should believe in Jesus because of certain blessings the Lord has given in their own, personal lives. "Jesus has given me such inner peace." "He has performed mighty miracles of healing in my family." "Christ has changed my life completely and has given me purpose and direction." "You should believe in Him, too, so you can have all these good things!"

The use of testimonials is one pitfall we should avoid, since it does not direct the listener to the Word of God and the objective Gospel. Another is the use of such phrases as "it seems to me," "I think this," etc. Such language gives the impression that religion is relative, and that it doesn't matter what you believe as long as you believe it.

We have two excellent examples in Holy Scripture of how to avoid such pitfalls. On the Day of Pentecost, when the disciples were given the promised Holy Spirit in special measure and received the gift of being able to speak in foreign languages, the apostle Peter preached a mighty sermon to the many Jews in the city of Jerusalem who were there for the great festival. He did not give a testimonial about how good he felt inside, nor did he speak about the blessings just outpoured by the Holy Spirit. Instead, Peter showed from Scripture that Jesus of Nazareth was the promised Messiah, the Christ (Acts 2:1-41).

In 1 Corinthians, the apostle Paul states clearly that the message of Jesus Christ is foolishness to the world. He, as Christ's ambassador, did not speak in eloquent words or show off some superior wisdom, but he simply proclaimed the message of "Jesus Christ and Him crucified," 1 Corinthians 1:18-2:5.

So as the Lord opens up doors for us to share His blessed Good News, may we speak with a firm "thus says the Lord," and not on the flimsy basis of our own opinions and experiences. As we tell others what God so clearly says in His inspired Word, may we also focus attention on the crucified and risen Jesus, who has earned forgiveness and eternal life for all.

SPECIFIC OPPORTUNITIES

Every day of our lives doors open up for us to say something about Jesus, and to apply the saving Gospel to the needs of our friends. In the following paragraphs, we have a listing of a few of these opportunities, and also some advice as to how to step through that open door.

1. TALKING ABOUT DEATH. Death is on everyone's mind, but it is something few people like to talk about. The subject arises with the terminally ill, the elderly, and those who have experienced the loss of a loved one. Young people feel that death is in the distant future for them, unless, of course, they have had a close call with death.

When others speak about death we can draw their attention quickly by saying, "I never plan to die." They'll respond with a surprised look and a question, and you can answer by saying, "Jesus says that He is the Resurrection and Life. He says that whoever believes in Him shall never die. Yes, my heart will stop and my body will lie cold in the grave, but my soul will be taken to heaven and on the Last

Day I will be raised from the dead and live with Jesus forever!"

2. SPEAKING OF THE TERRIBLE STATE IN WHICH THE
WORLD IS. More so today than ever before, people are in touch with what's going on around them. In nine out of ten conversations, the subjects of crime, natural disasters, wars, etc. arise. Very frequently it is expressed, "What's this world coming to?"

We can respond to such concerns by pointing out that the world has always been violent, and that such terrible things are the result of sin. It is then possible for us to point out how Jesus has washed away our sin in His blood, and that He has give to us a new heaven and a new earth to look forward to in His resurrection. A good way to involve the prospect in the religious portion of such a conversation is to ask a question like, "Even though this world is full of sin, isn't it wonderful the Savior has forgiven us?"

3. SPEAKING OF ANOTHER PERSON AS A CHRISTIAN. Many times when we gather with friends, we speak of mutual

acquaintances which are not present at the time. Other people often become a common subject of discussion (but be careful that you don't gossip!), and very frequently we hear it said of someone we know, "Oh, he's such a good Christian!"

What an excellent opportunity to speak of what a Christian really is! "Well, I consider myself a Christian, too," we can say. "But I know I'm not good. What I do know from the Bible is that I'm a sinner, but Jesus has forgiven me. Our church is not made up of good people, but sinners who find comfort and peace in the forgiveness of Jesus."

4. SPEAKING OF A SPECIAL PROBLEM OR NEED. If you have been discussing some problem or need that a person might have, many times you can point out from Scripture the solutions God has given to us. Here the importance of personal Bible study and meditation come into sharp focus.

But if the problem or need is not given a clear solution in the Bible, or if you are unfamiliar with what the Bible says about a certain subject, you can speak about our greatest problem---sin, and our greatest need---forgiveness. Here the Law and Gospel presentation which you prepared a few weeks ago would come in very handy.

5. WHEN LIFE SEEMS MEANINGLESS AND BORING. Most people today live in a spiritual vacuum---they don't know who they are, why they are here, or where they are going. When friends inform us of such despair in their own lives, we can respond by agreeing with them: "Yes, life often does appear that way." But don't leave it there. Continue by pointing out how life would really be if it were not for the cross and the empty grave of Christ, with the assurance they give to us of peace with God and eternal life.

CONCLUDING THE CONVERSATION

After each situation when a door has been opened for you to proclaim the Good News in relation to your friend's specific need, you can begin your Law and Gospel presentation. But also know when to stop. Don't end up boring people by rattling on and on. Don't repeat yourself, either---people hear what you have to say the first time! (Pastors, are you listening to this?) Say what you must, but then leave the rest to God the Holy Spirit to work through His Word. You can close the religious portion of your conversation by inviting the person and his family to church and Sunday school. It is also suggested that you keep some tracts or pamphlets handy in your home, car or purse. Also assure the person that he can always speak to you about such personal, spiritual matters in the strictest confidence, and that he is always welcome to speak to your pastor. When conversations reach such a point, or if the subject matter warrants it, please forward the person's name to the pastor so he can follow up.

EXERCISE

What would you say to such people in the following situations?

1) A friend of yours is going to stop going to his church because no spiritual comfort is offered in that church's ministry to its members.

2) Your neighbor's husband has just died, and

when you go over to her house to visit, the new widow breaks down in tears and cries, "Why did it have to happen?"

3) You visit a person you know in the hospital, and he has just been told by the doctor that he has contracted a terminal illness. He looks afraid, and expresses a very real fear of death.

4) A classmate gets involved with drugs and alcohol to a very deep extent, and he expresses the opinion that no one cares anymore, and that life is not worth living.

5) You're having lunch with some friends, and the topic of religion arises. Most express the opinion that Christianity is basically living a good, clean and upright life.

# LESSON EIGHT: RESPONDING TO EXCUSES

For centuries, men and women have given all sorts of excuses for not following Christ and His Word. In Luke 10:57-62, we behold the Savior calling men to follow Him. One offers the excuse that he must bury his dead father first. The other says he must go home and say "good-bye" to the folks.

Most excuses that are offered by people for not going to church are used to cover up a general animosity against God and what He has to say in His Word. By nature, human beings hate God. Romans 3:10-18 gives us a true description of our natural state.

It is only a miracle of God's grace that we put our trust in Jesus, and that we are assured that He has delivered us from sin, death and hell. As believing children of the heavenly Father, we want to share the Good News of Christ with others. But so often we run into excuses, hard-hearts, and stubbornness in the people with whom we speak. We wish to analyze today six excuses which are commonly given, and how to react to them.

We should realize that we respond to all excuses from a positive standpoint. People are turned off immediately when they sense they are looked down upon, or silently mocked, or are told what to do. Instead we should offer the sympathetic ear, show how we have often felt the same way, and then reveal the love and forgiveness of Christ in the Gospel.

SIX COMMON EXCUSES

1. THE CHURCH IS FULL OF HYPOCRITES. This is probably the most common excuse that is given for not going to church. Those who say this have probably had a bad experience in the past or in childhood, when they did go to church. They more than likely witnessed fellow members "act holier than thou" on Sunday morning, but then during the week saw them live their lives like the devil himself. Needless to say, such hypocrisy turned them off to organized religion.

How to respond: You might point out how Jesus, too, firmly condemned the hypocrisy of the scribes and the Pharisees, but that He also reached how for weak sinners who recognized their plight.  Show how Christ received and accepted the outcasts of society.  Reveal what Paul says in Romans 5:8, "While we were still sinners, Christ died for us."  You might also say something like, "You can't belong to our church if you aren't a sinner!"

2. I CAN WORSHIP GOD IN OTHER PLACES BESIDES A CHURCH BUILDING.  Many revise this excuse by saying, "I can worship God better out in the woods, or on the golf course, rather than in a church."

How to respond: It is true, we can worship God wherever we are and in whatever we do.  Our worship is not bound to a church building, but is to be reflected in our daily lives.  But that's only half the picture---the other half is God coming to us, strengthening our faith and comforting our hearts.  God does this through His Word and through the Lord's Supper.  All of this is done best in the worship service, for it is a rare time indeed when we actually sit down and meditate over what the Bible says.  And if we stay away from God's Word, our faith will eventually die, just as a human body will die if it is not fed.

3. SUNDAY IS THE ONLY DAY I HAVE TO SLEEP IN. Some put it this way: "Sunday is the only chance I have to spend with my family." Such an excuse reveals laziness and mixed-up priorities. When people feel this way they are in direct violation of the First Commandment, "Thou shalt have no other gods." They worship, instead of God, their bed, their family, or their recreation.

How to respond: Point out to the person the agitations of the week---the problems of home and work, difficulties with people, feelings of guilt and insufficiency. Show how our souls need rest just like our bodies. It might also do well to quote Jesus' words from Matthew 11:28, "Come unto Me, all ye who labor and are heavy laden, and I will give you rest." What better way is there to spend time with the family than in church?

4. I FELL TOO MUCH LIKE A SINNER WHEN I GO TO CHURCH; AND 5. THE PREACHER MAKES ME FEEL GUILTY. Such an excuse is frequently based on fact. In many fundamentalist churches, especially in the Bible Belt, being a Christian simply means that you don't have evil thoughts, you don't

swear, smoke or drink, and you tithe. In many pulpits all the preacher does is yell out fire and brimstone, telling his people that if they don't straighten up, they are headed straight for hell.

How to respond: We have here an excellent opportunity to share the Savior's love and forgiveness. You can use the Law and Gospel presentation you wrote out a few weeks ago. Point out that true Christianity consists in not what we do for God to earn our salvation, but what God did for us in Christ Jesus for our forgiveness. Show how Jesus takes us as we are---using the Biblical examples of David, Matthew, the prostitute, etc.

6. EVERYONE IGNORES ME. This excuse is often put another way: "No one talks to me when I go to church." People who use such an excuse are often the ones who don't speak to others. You can't have friends without being a friend. Sometimes this excuse is indeed based on fact, but most of the time the person is looking for an excuse not to go to church.

How to respond: Point out to the person that you can't have friends without being a friend, nor can you expect others to talk to you when you don't talk to them.  Also show that church is not a mere social function.  It is a time when God speaks to us in His Word and we speak to Him in prayer and praise.  And even if people do ignore us, Jesus listens and speaks to all!

CONCLUSION

There are many reasons for not going to church.  There are probably as many reasons as there are unchurched people.  We mentioned six of them here today---can you think of any more?  How would you respond?

## LESSON NINE: ASSIMILATING THE NEW MEMBER

### DEFINITION

Webster's dictionary defines the word "assimilate" this way: "To take something in and make it a part of oneself; absorb." When we speak of assimilating the new church member, we are referring to that ongoing process of making the person feel at home in his new church, and making sure he gets the utmost from that church's ministry.

An excellent Bible example of properly assimilating new members is recorded for us in Acts 2:42, "They devoted themselves to the apostles' teaching and to the fellowship, to the breaking of bread and to prayer." The "they" referred to in this verse are the 3,000 who were converted to Christ on the Day of Pentecost.

### HOW DO WE FOLLOW THE EXAMPLE OF THESE EARLIEST CHRISTIANS?

"They devoted themselves to the apostles' teaching..." Note how the inspired Word places training and instruction in the Word of God above all else.  The New Testament Books were in the process of being written, and how the new believers must have digested these Sacred Writings as soon as the ink dried on the paper!  How attentively they must have listened when given the opportunity to hear an apostle preach!

Even so today we emphasize to every new member the importance of Christian doctrine---a term we use for the teachings of Holy Scripture.  We encourage regular church, Sunday school and Bible class attendance, for a new convert (or an "old" Christian as well) cannot grow in his faith if he is not in touch with the Word (Cf. Romans 10:17).

"...And to the fellowship..."  This word "fellowship" does not merely refer to covered-dish suppers and ice-cream socials.  It signifies the unity and oneness of fellow believers in the one, true faith.  This "fellowship" which we have with like-minded believers is given evidence to in many ways---worshipping together, praying and communing together, confessing faith in the same Scriptural truths, loving one another as brothers and sisters in Christ, etc. We want the new member to realize he belongs---not just to our church, but also to the Holy Christian Church.

"...And to the breaking of bread..." Many Biblical commentators feel this phrase refers to the Lord's Supper. Not only did the early believers immerse themselves in the Scriptures and rejoice in their unity, but they also partook frequently of the Lord's Supper. Each communicant, whether young or old, should make use of this Sacrament often. It is one of the Means whereby God offers, gives and seals unto us the forgiveness of sins (Cf. 1 Corinthians 11:23-32).

"...And to prayer..." Our Savior comes to us in His love and mercy through the Gospel in Word and Sacraments. We come to Him with all of our wants, needs and praises in prayer. The new convert should be encouraged to use prayer, for in doing so he is exercising his privilege as a priest before God. Remember well the words to the popular hymn (TLH, #457):

What a Friend we have in Jesus,
All our sins and griefs to bear!
What a privilege to carry
Everything to God in prayer!
Oh, what peace we often forfeit,
Oh, what needles pain we bear,
All because we do not carry
Everything to God in prayer.

THE ONGOING PROCESS

A new convert doesn't find himself devoted to Christian doctrine, the fellowship, frequent participation at the Lord's Supper, and fervent prayer overnight. First there is the Instruction Class, where all the basic truths of the Bible are studied and discussed. Sometimes a baptism must be performed. Then there is the formal reception into membership during the Worship Service. All these things will happen if the Lord of the Church blesses our witnessing efforts with VISIBLE fruitfulness. But that is only the beginning! Besides those very important matters which we mentioned above, several other things must be brought to our attention which will help the new person feel right at home in our church.

1. EACH MEMBER MUST PERSONALLY WELCOME THE NEW PERSON. This is especially true in the small congregation. The newcomer must feel that he is a part of the congregation's family. That means getting him involved in church functions and activities. That means treating him as an individual, loving him as a fellow believer, helping him when he needs help, etc.

One of the most effective ways we can "quench the Spirit" and drown the fire in a new member is to make him feel left out. A person can feel left out even if he is involved in activities up to his neck! We can help people avoid feeling this way by talking to them, having fun with them, visiting with them, and helping them. In short, be a friend.

2. BE WILLING TO LISTEN TO AND ACCEPT NEW IDEAS. In many instances new members want to help in some way in the church. Maybe it's planning for a dinner, or working outside, etc. It is so easy out of politeness to say, "No, that's alright, you don't have to do it." But such a response again kills the fire and enthusiasm in the new member. Another temptation is to correct something a

new member has done in the church, or not to listen to his ideas on how something can be done better and more efficiently. How discouraged a person can become when everything he does out of love for his Lord is criticized or corrected because "it was never done that way before!" Let the new person speak up and get involved---isn't that what we should want?

3. BE PATIENT WITH THE NEW MEMBER'S SPIRITUAL UNDERSTANDING. There may be instances when a new member speaks up in a meeting, or in a class, and says something which we know is not quite right Scripturally. How easy it is for us to look down on that person, thinking we might have a heretic in our midst! How easy it would then be to accuse the pastor of not doing his job in the instruction class!

We must remember, however, that men who have been in the ministry for years don't "know it all." None of us will "know it all" until we reach heaven. How can we expect the new convert to know everything perfectly about Christian doctrine? When such an individual is willing to learn and listen, let's be patient, and give God's Word time to penetrate the heart.

CONCLUSION

In these past few weeks we have considered the whole evangelism spectrum---from what the Bible says about sharing the Gospel of Christ with others to concrete advice as to how to do so. Reread this program frequently. Refer to it again. May evangelism become a part of your everyday life!

**"For I am not ashamed of the gospel of Christ, for it is the power of God to salvation for everyone who believes, for the Jew first and also for the Greek. For in it the righteousness of God is revealed from faith to faith; as it is written, "The just shall live by faith," Romans 1:16-17.**

THINGS TO DO

1) Read and meditate over God's Word, the Bible, daily.

2) Pray for your pastor, congregation and church body.

3) Pray regularly for the unchurched and unbelieving people you know, asking the Savior to instruct their hearts with the Law and the Gospel.

4) Keep your ears constantly open for people crying for spiritual help, and always be ready to give them the Word.

5) Make regular use of your church's literature, giving it to people you know or with whom you have contact.

Made in the USA
Columbia, SC
26 October 2022